Original title:
A Christmas of Hope and Light

Copyright © 2024 Creative Arts Management OÜ
All rights reserved.

Author: Jaxon Kingsley
ISBN HARDBACK: 978-9916-94-040-2
ISBN PAPERBACK: 978-9916-94-041-9

Whispers of Winter's Glow

The snowflakes dance with glee,
As squirrels plot a heist for tea.
They'll steal your hat, oh what a sight,
While carolers sing with delight.

The trees are dressed in glittering white,
While snowmen grin with great delight.
They'll tell you jokes that make you snort,
And break the ice and all retort.

Lanterns in the Midnight Snow

The lanterns swing like jolly bells,
With Santa lost—he surely yells.
His reindeer munch on holiday treats,
While children giggle from their seats.

The midnight wind brings whistle tunes,
As moonlight shines on sleepy prunes.
They dream of toys and candy flakes,
While mom warns dad not to eat the cakes.

Rebirth of the Shining Stars

Stars twinkle like they know the joke,
As frosty breath makes all folks choke.
They hide behind the clouds to play,
And throw snowballs through the fray.

In snowy coats and mismatched socks,
We chase our pets and dodge the blocks.
With laughter ringing through the night,
We share hot cocoa, all feels right.

Frosty Dreams and Golden Wishes

The frost draws dreams on every pane,
While visions dance, they tease our brain.
A hamster wheel of wishful sight,
Where every moment feels so right.

The cookies vanish in one blink,
While folks all pause—and start to think.
Did Grandma bake them just for fun?
Or are they just an endless run?

Twinkling Spirits in the Cold

In the frost, we dance and play,
With jolly hats and bright display.
Snowmen wobble, scarf askew,
They laugh at us, and we laugh too.

Hot cocoa spills on my warm toes,
While reindeer steal my tasty prose.
Elves are giggling in the night,
They'll trip on tinsel, what a sight!

Beneath the Mistletoe's Kindness

Under the leaves, we squeal with glee,
A kiss for me or maybe three!
But wait—who's cousin is that guy?
I dodge the mistletoe so sly.

Grandma winks with mischief bright,
A sprig above, oh what a fright!
A cheeky peck turns into squeals,
As awkward hugs become new reels.

Illuminated Pathways of the Heart

Lines of lights wrap around the tree,
It's a sparkly mess, just wait and see!
Cats are climbing, chasing glow,
In a colorful light show below.

Neighbors shout and we reply,
"Behold our house, oh me, oh my!"
But deep inside we all just know,
Last year's garland's little glow.

A Fire Within the Frost

The fireplace crackles, warms our toes,
But someone's face begins to doze.
With marshmallows stuck in our hair,
We giggle as we start to share.

Grandpa's stories, oh how they flow,
Of sleigh rides taken way too slow.
With every laugh, the warmth ignites,
In the madness of our snowy nights.

The Season of Blessings and New Paths

In sweaters bright, we dance with glee,
As uncles munch on stollen, whee!
The lights are tangled in the tree,
A sight so funny, can you see?

With cookie crumbs upon the floor,
The cat's now wrestling with the store.
A gift that squeaks, oh what a score!
It's chaos wrapped in cheer galore!

The snowflakes float like disco balls,
While Grandma laughs and slightly falls.
Our holiday spirit gently calls,
To joy that fills our festive halls.

In every laugh a joy we find,
A family gathering, one of a kind.
With hearts all warm and purely kind,
New paths unfold, let love unwind.

Harmonic Whispers of the Holiday Spirit

The carolers sing off-key, it's true,
While children shove snowballs at my shoe.
My Auntie jigs to a tune so blue,
We dance and laugh, what else to do?

Lights twinkle like some cosmic bling,
While the turkey's doing the cha-cha thing.
We all join in, our voices ring,
In this crazy fun, our hearts take wing.

The dog dons a hat that's way too tight,
He spins and barks, oh what a sight!
With every hug, the mood feels right,
Together we shine, oh so bright.

With laughter echoing all around,
Each silly story, a joy profound.
In festive chaos, peace is found,
Harmonic whispers, our hearts unbound.

The Joy of Being Home

The cookies burned, the kids are wild,
The dog's wearing a hat, looking mild.
The lights are tangled, what a sight,
But laughter fills the cozy night.

With slippers mismatched and hot cocoa spills,
We're warm in our chaos, with holiday frills.
Each silly mishap adds to the cheer,
We embrace the absurd, there's nothing to fear.

Illuminated Aspirations Under Festive Skies

The stars blink down, winking with glee,
While uncle Fred fights the tree like a bee.
Each ornament's story is tangled in laughs,
As we dodge falling branches with humorous gaffes.

Outside snowflakes dance, but inside we brawl,
Over which treat is the best of them all.
With jokes and with joy in every warm tale,
We raise up our mugs to the holiday hail.

A Gathering of Warm Wishes

The doorbell's ringing, it's a neighbor's cat,
He stole our last muffin, imagine that!
We've dressed up the house with odd little things,
Like mismatched socks and bright paper wings.

With friends in pajamas, we toast with delight,
To moments of chaos that feel just right.
Every hug holds the warmth like a bright inner song,
In a world full of laughter where we all belong.

The Light that Guides Us Through

The candles flicker as grandma winks,
She tells us her stories while the puppy drinks.
The lessons of laughter, the friendships we mold,
When chaos surrounds, warmth is pure gold.

With a pie on the floor and giggles that rise,
We cherish the moments, the funny surprise.
United we stand, like mismatched socks,
Together we shine, in our own little box.

Snowy Fields of Rejuvenation

Snowflakes drift like fluff on a chair,
I slipped and flopped—oh, what a scare!
Penguins slide with grace, I'm left behind,
Wishing I had wings, oh how I whined!

Giddy laughter echoes through the snow,
My snowman's a monster, don't let him grow!
Hot cocoa spills as friends start to play,
Can't catch a breath, so we laugh all day!

Brilliance in the Blanket of White

Twinkling lights wrap houses in cheer,
While squirrels ponder, 'Is that my snack here?'
I lost my mitten, it's quite the sight,
Now just a glove, it's lost in the night!

Snowball fights turn into big mush,
Friends are all laughing, causing a hush.
Rolling in snow, I made a big mess,
But joy's in the chaos, I must confess!

The Light of Giving in a World of Cold

Presents wrapped in paper, all bright and fun,
Cats chase ribbons, we can't even run!
Laughter erupts as I trip on a chair,
Who knew a gift could cause such a scare?

Cookies are baking, oh what a treat!
But dough on my face? That's hard to beat!
The reindeer are prancing, all in a row,
While I'm stuck inside, watching the show!

Together We Shine Through December

Gathered with loved ones, all snug and tight,
We tell hilarious tales that last through the night.
The candles flicker, shadows dance on the wall,
As I snag the last cookie — oh, silly me, tall!

In cozy pajamas, we bicker and play,
Guess who knocked over the tree in dismay?
But smiles are plenty, the warmth feels so grand,
Together we sparkle, united we stand!

Threads of Joy in a Silent World

In a land where reindeer dance,
Elves juggle gifts, take a chance.
Snowmen wear the silliest hats,
Chasing cats, the grumpy spats.

Mittens lost and socks gone rogue,
Hot cocoa makes us all a vogue.
Twinkling lights in tangled mess,
Who knew joy could be such stress?

Carols sung with off-key cheer,
Bells ring out, but who can hear?
Laughter bubbles, like fizzy drinks,
A day of joy with silly winks.

Through snowflakes, wishes take to flight,
In this world, there shines so bright.
Wrapped in warmth, we find our cheer,
With every giggle, love draws near.

Echoes of Love in Snowflakes

Once I tripped on candy canes,
Fell right down, now here I reign.
Snowflakes land upon my nose,
I laugh out loud, that's how it goes!

Gingerbread, oh how it crumbles,
With sweet icing, our laughter doubles.
Cats in hats, dogs in bows,
Everywhere, our joy just flows.

Hallways echo, laughter's song,
Who would guess this day feels long?
Mistakes made, like burnt-up pies,
But oh, the love is no surprise!

Underneath the mistletoe,
Kisses given to those we know.
In this frosty, funny whirl,
A jolly heart begins to twirl.

Radiant Wishes on Darkest Days

When the lights go dim and low,
We light our lamps, our spirit's glow.
Cookies baked, but oh, they burnt,
Yet still we laugh, our hearts are turned.

Funny sweaters, patterns clash,
With reindeer leaping — what a bash!
Kids in snowdrifts, falling free,
Who knew joy could be so goofy?

Amidst the ice, we find our grace,
Chasing each other in a race.
With silly games and holiday cheer,
We make our funny memories here.

So gather 'round the sparkling light,
Sharing giggles, hearts so bright.
In every moment, don't despair,
Love's warmth surrounds us everywhere.

A Tapestry of Warm Embrace

As we craft our holiday threads,
With tangled yarns and random spreads.
A scarf goes round, but what's this fuss?
It ends up as a cozy bus!

Goblins hide in wrapping paper,
While grandpa sports a paper taper.
With mistletoe that swings too low,
Kisses given in a comical flow.

Hot dogs dressed like candy canes,
Strange delights, oh what remains?
We juggle fruitcake, laughs collide,
Even the cat takes it in stride.

In cozy corners, stories spun,
With all our blunders, we have fun.
Every embrace, a warm surprise,
In this tapestry, love never lies.

Seasons of Kindness Wrapped in Time

In December's chill, we find our cheer,
With cookies that dance, oh what a smear!
The snowmen grin, wearing hats too tight,
While squirrels debate if they'll start a fight.

The carolers sing, but one is off-key,
As reindeer prance with a clumsy spree.
Yet laughter erupts like hot cocoa spills,
Uniting us all in the jolly thrills.

Flickers of Peace in the Winter Solstice

The candles flicker, they flicker and sway,
While dad tells tales from his wild younger days.
Uncle Joe dons a hat far too bright,
And grandma's still feisty, ready to fight.

We dance by the tree, tripping on toes,
The cat steals the tinsel as everyone doze.
In a flurry of joy, we all raise a toast,
To the moments that matter, our magical most!

Dreams Adrift on Slumbering Snow

Snowflakes tumble like clumsy clowns,
While families gather in cozy towns.
The kids build forts, then throw snow with might,
As hot drinks spill in a caffeinated fight.

The stars twinkle like grandmas' bright brooch,
And laughter echoes, a sweet, funny roach.
We dream in warmth, as the world fades away,
In a blanket of joy, we frolic and play.

Ember Hearts in the Frosty Night

With logs in the fire, our spirits revive,
A band of misfits, yet we all thrive.
The mistletoe's up, caught in a glitch,
Dad nearly falls, oh what a big pitch!

The dog joins the fun, trying to skate,
With socks on his paws, oh, isn't it great!
As marshmallows toast and stories unfold,
We cherish the warmth more than silver or gold.

Cinnamon Dreams and Candlelight

In the kitchen, scents collide,
Cinnamon swirls with dough inside.
Cookies dance, oh what a sight,
Sprinkled sugar, pure delight.

The cat knocks down the candy canes,
While I hum old holiday refrains.
Eggnog spills, it's quite the show,
Who knew cooking could overflow?

Children giggle, make a mess,
Wrapping paper, I must confess:
Presents hidden behind the tree,
A life-size elf? Just wait and see!

As we gather, laughter beams,
In our hearts, the spirit gleams.
With twinkling eyes and silly hats,
Let's spread the joy like jumping cats!

Embracing the Wonderland Within

Snowflakes tumble, hats awry,
Snowmen with an extra eye.
Sleds go flying, what a thrill,
Watch out, here comes "Runaway Bill!"

Mittens mismatched on each hand,
Everyone slips, not quite as planned.
Hot cocoa with marshmallows supreme,
But watch out! They float – what a dream!

A snowball fight, who's got the flair?
One hit's mom – oh, that's not fair!
Laughter echoes, a joyful sound,
As we tumble on the frosty ground.

With sparkly lights that dance and shine,
We celebrate with friends and wine.
Embracing winter's clumsy charms,
We'll keep each other safe from harms!

Flickers of Joy Among the Pines

Trees adorned with lights and cheer,
Every corner holds some beer.
Nuts and bolts from last year's fix,
People tripping on their own tricks.

The dog runs off, the cat's a blur,
Under the table, there's the spur.
Boughs hang low with so much glee,
Just don't let grandma spill her tea!

Laughter echoes, oh what a mix,
Of buttered yams and candy sticks.
We toast to joy, with nibbles galore,
And hints of laughter from the floor.

Flickers of joy in every nook,
With each mishap, I just can't look.
But oh, the warmth of love's sweet glow,
Makes every blunder part of the show!

A Symphony of Light in the Silence

Twinkling lights set the scene,
As we dance like fools, oh so keen.
The holidays bring so much clamor,
But who's counting? We're full of glamor!

A choir starts, not quite in tune,
Is that Grandma singing a cartoon?
Pajamas jive, socks mismatched,
In this chaos, joy has hatched.

With every giggle, joy ignites,
The jokes we share become our heights.
In the silence, we craft our cheer,
With each little moment, we draw near.

As snowflakes twirl and spirits rise,
We create our own funny skies.
This symphony, a crooked score,
But our hearts sing out, forevermore!

Festive Flames of Friendship

Gingerbread houses built with care,
Frosting on the roof, though it's rare.
Friends with whiskers, tails, and cheer,
Nibbling on cookies, oh dear, oh dear!

Twinkling lights on every dim tree,
Jingle bells jingling just for me.
Neighbors in pajamas, what a sight,
Singing carols, trying to get it right.

Hot cocoa spills on the holiday floor,
Marshmallows floating, and there's more!
Laughter echoes through the chilly night,
Embracing moments, oh what a delight!

Wrapping up gifts all mismatched and bright,
Mistletoe hanging, hearts feeling light.
The flames are dancing, the chaos is grand,
In this festive season, together we stand.

Illumination in the Dark

Candles flicker in the night air,
Shadows dancing without a care.
Baking cookies, oh what a mess,
Flour everywhere, it's anyone's guess!

Strings of lights wrapped round the cat,
He thinks it's a toy, not so daft!
Neighbors gather, all tales and tease,
'The turkey's gone rogue!' someone agrees.

Pine needles on the carpet stick tight,
Ho-ho-hoing echoes, a comical sight.
Socks mismatched, joy running wild,
In this nutty season, we're all just a child.

And when the power flickers out,
We'll laugh and sing, without a doubt.
Bright stars above as the moon peeks in,
In the darkest hours, let the fun begin!

Tidings of Joy and Serenity

Snowflakes flutter like tiny kites,
Snowmen rugged up, embracing the nights.
Sledding down hills that giggle and sway,
'Who knew winter could be such play?'

Friends in hats that seem too tight,
Trying to balance in a snowball fight.
Giggles and grumbles mix in the air,
Mittens mismatched, turning chaos to fair.

Cider simmering, the scent draws us near,
Sipping with friends, spreading the cheer.
Laughter erupts, as stories unfold,
We treasure these memories, forever retold.

Wrapping up laughter in twinkling lights,
Joy bursting forth with cozy delights.
In this season, when smiles are so grand,
We hold each other's hearts in a hand.

The Spirit of Giving

Candies and treats all piled high,
'Don't eat them all!' No one can deny.
Secret Santa swaps in a laughing crowd,
Caution? Unheard of, laughter too loud!

Cards that get lost, a gift gone astray,
Surprises are better when they come this way.
The dog chews on bows, oh what a thief,
While all we can do is laugh in disbelief.

Decorating trees nearly went wrong,
Tinsel tangles; it can take long.
Yet giggles prevail as ornaments drop,
It's the fun in the making that never will stop.

With hugs and smiles, our spirits ignite,
From giving and sharing, oh what a sight.
Fumbling our way in the joy we create,
With laughter and warmth, let's celebrate!

Glowing Paths to New Horizons

In the dark where shadows creep,
We find our joy in laughter's leap.
With silly hats and socks of red,
We dance around, forget the dread.

Twinkling lights on every street,
Behind each door, a merry greet.
Hot cocoa spills, a marshmallow dive,
Who knew that chaos helps us thrive?

The Brightness of Love in the Dark

A cat in a scarf, oh what a sight,
Purring softly by candlelight.
While cookies bake and laughter flows,
We trade our secrets, the best of prose.

With frosty breath, we sing off-key,
A tune that shimmers, wild and free.
The night's embrace, so warm and bold,
In a world of delight, we won't fold.

Stars in the Eyes of Dreamers

With every wish upon a star,
We giggle like we've gone too far.
Snowflakes tumble, a waltzing cheer,
We'll bake our troubles far and near.

The reindeer sledge, a clattering show,
Who knew they'd dance, stealing the glow?
With tinsel tangled in our hair,
We laugh until we can't bear.

Heartstrings Bound by Holiday Cheer

Through pine-scented halls, we prance,
While Uncle Joe attempts to dance.
His two left feet, a laugh parade,
Lost in joy, we won't trade.

With every bauble on the tree,
A wink, a grin, so carefree.
We deck the halls without a care,
With goofy grins and socks we wear.

The Warmth Beneath the Ice

The snowflakes dance like they are bold,
In mittens too small, we all feel cold.
With cocoa in hand, and marshmallows galore,
We laugh at the penguins who knock on the door.

The sleds are racing, but we take a fall,
The snowman's got class; we're just having a ball.
In frozen terrain, we scream with delight,
Who knew ice could bring us so much silly fright?

Glittering Hearts in Quiet Nights

The stars are twinkling, they seem to play,
While we try to sing in a funny way.
But carols are tricky, notes seem to flee,
Good thing my voice sounds like a buzzing bee!

The cookies are baking, they smell divine,
Yet half of them vanish, it's all quite fine.
With sprinkles that rain like colorful snow,
We giggle and munch, then yell, "Oh no!"

Candles Flicker, Spirits Rise

The candles are flickering, what a great sight,
But one jumps in shock, and starts a small fright.
With laughter and joy, we cover our eyes,
As the room fills up with our quirky surprise.

The table is set with a feast so grand,
But dinner takes off like it's not in our hands.
We chase after turkey that rolls down the hall,
The chase turns into quite the comical hall ball.

Embracing the Chill with Cheer

The frost on the window creates a clear scene,
Of snowmen and sleds, and a big tangerine.
With mittens that mismatch, we dance in a line,
Our feet make a symphony, oh what a time!

The chilly air sparkles, it tickles our nose,
As we giggle and chortle through frosty snows.
With cheeks all aglow and spirits so high,
We embrace the winter, not knowing why!

The Light We Share in Winter's Grip

In winter's chill, we gather round,
With hot cocoa to be found.
Mittens lost and socks askew,
We laugh at what we thought we knew.

Twinkling lights on every tree,
Bright enough for all to see.
The neighbor's cat took quite a leap,
And landed right in Mary's heap!

Snowflakes tumble, soft and white,
Missed my hat—it took a flight!
Chasing it, oh what a sight,
Two kids tangled, what a plight!

But still we smile, in bitter cold,
With stories, jokes, and warmth to hold.
Together here, our spirits soar,
It's brighter now, who could want more?

Stories of Hope Beneath the Stars

Beneath the sky, the stars are bright,
We trade our tales, our laughs ignite.
Uncle Joe, with stories grand,
Of his old sleigh that slipped on sand.

Percy's dog chased after ducks,
Scaring away our Christmas clucks.
We giggle as we gaze above,
Finding joy in every shove.

With marshmallows on the fire,
We roast our dreams and never tire.
Cousin Sue's strange dance routine,
Has us all giggling, it's obscene!

So under stars, we spin our yarns,
Of snowball fights and slips on lawns.
Each story shared, a glowing spark,
In winter's dark, we leave our mark.

Peace Blossoms in the Snow

As snowflakes swirl around the room,
I trip and fall right near the broom.
Peaceful moments can't go wrong,
Though I'm now stuck in a song!

Mittens fly like little birds,
Then tangled up in silly words.
We barter cookies, pie for cake,
A peace treaty for dessert's sake!

Kids tie ribbons on the cat,
Who sprawls out flat—a furry mat.
Our laughter blooms like flowers bright,
In frosty air, it feels just right.

And so we toast with sparkling cheer,
To friends and fun and love held dear.
The snow may fall, but here we glow,
With peace and jokes beneath the snow.

Beneath the Holly's Gentle Touch

Under holly sprigs we find our way,
Singing tunes that lead astray.
With jingle bells all out of tune,
Our harmony's a comical swoon.

The mistletoe hung way too high,
So I just waved and slipped on by.
Who knew romance could take a dive?
With each attempt, we thrive, we strive!

Gifts wrapped up with tape galore,
Clumsy fingers, oh what a chore!
What's in the box—a rubber chicken?
It seems my gift game needs some kickin'!

But laughter sparkles, bright and clear,
Beneath the merry, festive cheer.
Though mishaps might give us a crutch,
We cradle joy beneath the touch.

Softly Sparkling Through the Silence

Twinkling lights dance on the trees,
Gaily chuckling with the breeze.
Snowflakes swirl like a cotton ball,
Even the grumpy cat is in thrall.

Hot cocoa spills on Auntie Sue,
Mirthful giggles, 'What to do?'
A silly hat on Grandpa's head,
Who knew he could be a fashion spread?

Muffins rise and the oven pings,
Sing-alongs and wobbly swings.
The dog joins in to steal a treat,
How can such chaos feel so sweet?

Through the frosty air it glows,
A warmth that everyone knows.
With a wink and a belly laugh,
The season's joy is a perfect gaff.

Gentle Hopes Breathe in the Air

Gentle whispers float on high,
Joyful spirits as we sigh.
Sprinkles of cheer on every stranger,
With laughter, we'll dance around the danger.

Cookies crumble in a jolly mess,
Who placed the flour? We must confess.
Floating wishes on a gingerbread,
Topping dreams with icing spread.

Stockings hung with mismatched flair,
One for the dog; no, that's not fair!
Elf hats squish on everyone's heads,
As we race to see who went to bed.

Bubbling laughter fills the room,
Disappearing, then back with a zoom.
Unexpected joy breaks like dawn,
With light and smiles, we will carry on.

The Glow of Togetherness

Around the table, a feast we share,
Where Grandma's stories are full of flair.
With each tale, a giggle grows,
As everyone adds their own prose.

Lights that twinkle bring silly cheer,
Helping the shy ones draw near.
Impromptu dance-offs take the stage,
Too much eggnog, they just engage!

Cards and gifts, wrapped with care,
Surprises hidden everywhere.
A mischievous cat on the tablecloth,
Oh no, look out! Here comes the froth!

In this warmth, our hearts align,
With funny faces, we sip our wine.
Through merry chaos, the night ignites,
In the glow of love, everything's right.

Lantern Light Against the Darkness

Lanterns flicker, casting fun,
A game of hide and seek begun.
While shadows jump, we laugh with glee,
Even the trees want to join the spree.

With scarves wrapped tight against the chill,
Uncle Joe attempts to do a thrill.
He trips on the step, a comical fall,
While we erupt into joyful brawl.

The stars twinkle like they are friends,
Joining us as the daylight ends.
Each twinkling promise, a funny sight,
Bringing warmth and joy to the night.

So let the lanterns glow a bit,
While we dance our way through the skit.
Darker nights may bring some fright,
But laughter always shines so bright.

Glimmers of Faith in the Chill

In the frosty air, we glide,
Snowflakes dancing side by side.
With a mitten on my nose,
I chuckle at how winter goes.

The hot cocoa's not too hot,
Marshmallows bouncing like a tot.
We laugh 'til we can't breathe,
Wishing for a warm reprieve.

Lights are tangled, oh what a sight,
A cat's playing hide-and-seek tonight.
Twinkling bulbs all on the floor,
I guess we'll just buy some more!

In the chill, we find our cheer,
With giggles ringing clear and near.
Sledding down slopes, oh what a thrill,
Finding joy in every chill.

Radiant Laughter in Snowfall

Snowflakes tickle on my chin,
As I try to build a win.
My snowman's really quite unique,
One eye's a button, one's a leak.

Building forts, we launch the snow,
With laughter echoing below.
"Missed me, missed me!" shouts the crew,
But I'll get you with my snowball too!

Hot pies smelling from the oven,
Grandma's secret – all are lovin'.
But when I taste, it's leaves instead,
The laugh erupts, I drop my head.

With twinkling lights, we sing away,
Off-key tunes brighten up the gray.
In every flurry, we find delight,
Who knew snow could spark such light?

The Gift of Togetherness

Gather 'round this merry tree,
I brought the fruitcake, oh dear me!
It's so dense, a bear could lift,
Yet somehow, it's our favorite gift.

All my cousins dance around,
With crazy socks and laughter sound.
The dog is dressed as Santa's elf,
I swear he's got more style than myself.

Presents come with funky bows,
Wrapped in paper that nearly glows.
But when she opens it, oh my lord,
It's a potato, not a reward!

In this chaos, love unfolds,
Through goofy stories, laughter molds.
Together here, our hearts ignite,
In silly moments, pure delight.

Echoes of Christmas Cheer

The snowmen wink from the lawn,
As we sing our way to dawn.
A tree adorned with socks and ties,
Even the raccoons share our fries.

Grandpa's jokes are quite the hit,
As he juggles, we can't sit.
"Why did the turkey cross the street?"
"Because he saw the stuffing's treat!"

We spill popcorn, filling the space,
It's flying everywhere - what a race!
But the cat thinks it's a game, oh dear,
We're all together, holiday cheer.

So let the echo's ring with glee,
With laughter shared by all, you see.
In the warmth of love, we find our flare,
Through funny moments, we all care.

The Glow of Unity and Love

In a cozy house, laughter rings,
With sweaters tight, and hats that sing.
A cat in a tree, oh what a sight,
As ornaments tumble, oh what a fright!

Cookies are baking, flour's in the air,
Mom slips and slides, with grace quite rare.
Dad cracks a joke, the punchline so grand,
It's stuck in the chimney—will it ever land?

We gather 'round with mugs in hand,
Hot cocoa spills—oh, it wasn't planned!
Gifts wrapped in bows that are way too tight,
We swap and giggle, it's pure delight!

Laughter glows, like stars up above,
In joyful chaos, we find our love.
With silly hats and hugs galore,
Together we cherish, forevermore.

Joy in the Heartbeat of Winter

Snowflakes dance and tickle my nose,
Winter's chill, but laughter grows.
A snowman's hat makes a great surprise,
When it rolls away before our eyes!

We sled down hills with squeals of glee,
Landing in snow, oh what a spree!
Hot chocolate mustaches all around,
Giggles erupt, what joy we've found!

The fireplace crackles, it sings a tune,
As Auntie's turkey takes flight like a balloon.
The dog steals a snack—what a cheeky thief!
We laugh and protest, but it's pure relief!

The rhythm of winter, a joyful beat,
Where mishaps turn to moments sweet.
Together we cherish every little thing,
In this winter wonder, oh how we sing!

Candlelit Wishes on Frosted Windows

Candle lights flicker, shadows play,
Grandma spills cider, oh what a ballet!
Frosted windows, the artwork flows,
As mischief unfolds, like a winter show!

A dog in a sweater, what a fine beast,
He promptly escapes, a frosty feast!
We chase him down through the snowy ground,
With laughter and giggles, true joy we've found!

Above us, twinkle lights brightly gleam,
While Uncle Joe's jokes are a far-off dream.
He tells a tall tale that's full of cheer,
But somehow it always comes around here!

In candlelit wishes, our hearts ignite,
Sharing sweet secrets on that glorious night.
With cookie crumbs scattered, we end our quest,
In love and laughter, we feel so blessed.

The Serenity of Family Gatherings

Family's together, the vibe is pure,
With hugs and chaos, it's quite the tour.
Dad's telling stories, half of it's true,
The other half's lost in grandma's stew!

On the table, a feast like no other,
A turkey that looks like it has a mother.
We pass the potatoes, a slippery slide,
As Aunt May's laughter fills up the wide.

Games are erupting, from charades to pie,
As cousin Sam pretends to fly high.
We snicker and chortle at his grand parade,
An unforgettable moment, perfectly made!

As evening draws near, we gather and sing,
With hearts all aglow, what joy does it bring!
The serenity found in this playful embrace,
Is love at its finest, a treasured space.

Sparkling Light in the Midwinter

In December's chill, we brave the snow,
With every flake, our laughter grows.
A jolly elf slipped on the ice,
His belly jiggled—oh, so nice!

Twinkling lights on every street,
A festive dance with two left feet.
Grandma's pie, oh what a treat,
But watch for crumbs beneath your seat!

The carolers sing with joyous cheer,
But off-key notes might burst your ear.
Still, we smile and sway along,
To the wobbly tune of holiday song!

Snowmen wobble, noses askew,
One lost his hat and we all knew.
With carrot noses and hats too tight,
They dance and grin in the warm moonlight!

Hope Wrapped in Warmth

A fire crackles, shadows play,
Uncle Joe burns the socks—oh, yay!
We gather close all wrapped in cheer,
With stories that we love to hear.

Bright ribbons twist around each gift,
But careful now, my wrapping's a lift!
It looks like something from a wild fight,
Yet we'll unwrap with pure delight.

Hot chocolate spills on grandma's knee,
A moment of joy, oh can't you see?
She laughs it off, with a twinkle bright,
"Who needs a mug? I could use a bite!"

Outside the wind makes funny sounds,
Like Santa's sleigh with squeaky bounds.
We hear his laugh from far away,
And gather round to shout hooray!

Evergreen Dreams and Silver Linings

A tree adorned in sparkly flair,
With mismatched ornaments laid with care.
A cat climbs high, then takes a leap,
Down goes the star—oh what a heap!

Pine-scented joys, mixed with cheer,
But watch your step, there's tinsel near!
With every bead on the carpet stuck,
We laugh and declare, "Oh, what bad luck!"

Cookie dough fights are all the rage,
Frosted messes on every page.
With sprinkles flying like confetti bright,
We taste and giggle, oh what a sight!

The days are short, but smiles are wide,
With every blunder, we beam with pride.
We find our joy in little things,
Like broken bulbs and silly flings!

Unity Beneath the Winter Moon

Under the moon, we gather near,
With woolly hats and festive cheer.
A snowball flies—oh what a aim,
Watch for the one who shouts your name!

Around the fire, stories flow,
With tall tales that make our faces glow.
Uncle Bob's fish is way too big,
Who sees the truth? It's all in the jig!

Marshmallows roast with a singed delight,
Oh, they're tasty, but not quite right.
Burnt edges make us laugh and sigh,
It's the best thing—don't even ask why!

We join our voices, off-key and bold,
Singing of warmth through winter's cold.
With friends like these, by the fire's light,
We find our joy, the world feels right!

Gathering of Souls Around the Fire

Gather round feet near the flames,
Stories shared, but none are the same.
Marshmallow fluff in a sticky fight,
Laughter echoes deep into the night.

Socks mismatched, oh what a sight,
Comfy chairs in the soft twilight.
Ghosts in the corner, are they just a joke?
Or did Uncle Joe really choke on smoke?

Hot cocoa spills down a cheeky grin,
Tiny elves plotting mischief within.
The fire crackles, we roast our fate,
As we bicker who's late to the plate.

Gathered 'round, let merriment swell,
In this warm tale, all is well.
Jokes are flung like pinecones high,
Under the glow of a starlit sky.

Wrapped in Cheer and Memories

Bows on the presents, not tied too neat,
Unwrap the glory, feel the heat!
Socks from Grandma, what a real treat,
With holes that sing 'I've walked on my feet!'

Cookies stacked high, looking so sweet,
But Auntie's secret? They taste like beet!
With every bite, a chuckle ignites,
As we wonder where she got her sights.

Photo frames full, memories alive,
Fuzzy sweaters that somehow survive.
Each hug and grin, time's magic show,
Wrapped in cheer, like a cozy glow.

The lights twinkle bright and dance with flair,
Making us laugh 'til we gasp for air.
Old stories retold, in fits of cheer,
Memories wrapped, evergreen dear.

The Dance of Snowflakes and Spirits

Snowflakes waltz and take their turn,
While snowmen plot their frosty yearn.
With carrot noses, they laugh and fold,
As snowball fights get stories retold.

The wind whispers with a giggle or two,
As hats fly off, oh what a view!
Chasing each other in a snow-filled spree,
Someone's lost a glove, and it's not just me!

Spirits rising, the cocoa's hot,
Laughter bubbles, in every pot.
Dance with the flakes, let joy take the stage,
Embracing the warmth while we act our age.

Beneath the stars, we twirl around,
As snowflakes and giggles make the sound.
Together we spin in a festive delight,
Creating our memories, shining so bright.

Remembering the Shimmer of Yesteryear

Digging through boxes, such a grand find,
Old ornaments tangled, a true rewind.
With each shiny bauble, a story unfolds,
Of laughter and mishaps, each one never old.

The tinsel's a mess, but we don't care,
How it twinkled and danced, in the living room air.
We laugh at the photos, hairstyles bizarre,
Uncle Bob dressed as Santa, a real rock star!

The memories taunt us, with playful glee,
Of mishaps when baking, oh dearie me!
With a pinch of laughter, and a dash of fun,
We stitch together tales 'til the day is done.

So raise up your glasses, toast to it all,
To shimmer and laughter, we'll answer the call.
In the glow of the night, let joy reappear,
Remembering the magic of yesteryear.

Frosted Memories and Warm Promises

Snowflakes dance like tiny sprites,
Twirling through the chilly nights.
Cookie crumbs on the floor,
I hear Santa's laugh, maybe more!

The tree's so tall, it touches skies,
With lights that blink and catch my eyes.
Mom's hot cocoa's sweet and thick,
Yet spills on Dad, oh what a trick!

Grandpa's snoring on the chair,
While dog steals his hat without a care.
Laughter echoes through the hall,
As we share stories, one and all.

The snowman winks with a goofy grin,
His carrot nose slants, it feels like a win.
In this season, we find delight,
Finding joy through cold, frosty nights.

A Hearth of Hope in the Quiet Cold

Socks so big they fit my cat,
He struts around, thinkin' he's a brat.
The fireplace crackles, sparks fly high,
I roast marshmallows, oh my, oh my!

The puppy paws at my sleeping feet,
Dreaming of snacks and something sweet.
A sock on his head, it makes him look tough,
But he's just a softie, in puffs of fluff.

The snow outside piles up with glee,
Making forts that hide each kid and me.
We throw snowballs, laughter's in the air,
'Cause who needs manners when snow's everywhere?

As the clock ticks down to midnight fun,
I hope the season's just begun.
Through the cold, we glow with cheer,
With warm hearts bounding, year after year.

Twinkling Dreams of the Evening Star

Stars are twinkling all ablaze,
Like disco balls, they daze and amaze.
I spot Rudolph, is that him there?
Delivering gifts with flair and care?

The reindeer prance on rooftops higher,
While kids below chant songs of fire.
Grandma in her slippers does a little jig,
As she makes room for every big fig!

The cat chases glitter from the tree,
While the dog ponders his next great spree.
Tinsel flies as a ribbon's snatched,
It's a party now, this chaos unmatched!

Here's to giggles, shenanigans, and cheer,
With each shining star, it's crystal clear.
Joy fills our hearts, and spirits soar high,
In this festive air, we never say goodbye.

Warmth in the Winter Whisper

The cold wind howls, a silly tune,
While snowflakes swirl like a cartoon.
Kids in sleds race down the hill,
With cheers and giggles, they can't sit still!

Hot pies baking in the oven nice,
But beware of the cat who thinks they're spice.
Grandpa's joke is a bit too corny,
A festive chuckle, never too thorny!

The lights outside blink wildly bright,
We stargaze and giggle at their fright.
Each moment splashes with colors so bold,
Creating stories that never grow old.

As we gather close in this merry scene,
Our laughter dances, our hearts are keen.
With joy all around, pathways to ignite,
We savor it all, this season's delight.

Threads of Hope in the Fabric of Winter

Amidst the snowflakes, we twirl and spin,
Our mittens too small, let the fun begin!
Hot cocoa spills as we giggle and cheer,
Even the snowmen join in our sneer.

The woolen scarf tangled, we laugh and sigh,
I think I just lost my shoe, oh dear, my!
But in the frost, we embrace the cold,
With friends by our side, warmth we behold.

A snowball fight breaks with a splatter and thud,
Hats fly off, landing right in the mud!
With laughter ringing through the yonder night,
These threads of joy weave our hearts so bright.

So let the winter winds blow and whirl,
With each silly slip, let the laughter unfurl.
For in this chill, our spirits do soar,
Hand in hand, we'll hope for even more!

Hope Rising Like the Morning Sun

Awake and stretch, it's time to rise,
With mischief twinkling in sleepy eyes.
The toast is burnt, but who cares today?
We'll just spread jam a creative way!

The sun peeks in like a cheerful chap,
"Wear your bright socks!" I heard him clap.
With mismatched mittens, we dash outside,
Catch me if you can, oh what a ride!

It's snowing glitter on this fun-filled morn,
Chasing our hopes, a new day is born.
Each snowflake twirls like a whirling spoon,
We'll dance through this winter, oh what a tune!

So here we go, let's greet the sky,
With giggles and play, time will surely fly.
The warmth in our hearts, it beams so bright,
Wherever we wander, all will be right!

Kindled Hearts in the Chill of December

In the chill of night, with cookies in tow,
We dash to the tree, don't spill the cocoa!
With ornament fights and the tinsel strung,
Each blunder we make, our laughter has sprung.

The fireplace crackles, a comedic play,
As the cat scales the tree in a crazy ballet.
We chase him with giggles, as he gives a meow,
Finding a cozy spot; oh, what a plow!

Our hearts are aglow with stories we share,
Of mishaps and laughter, of memories rare.
With each little flicker, our joy takes flight,
In the cold of December, we shine ever bright.

So let's toast to moments, both silly and dear,
With kindness and warmth, we gather near.
In this winter wonder, our spirits entwine,
For joy is the gift that we all keep divine!

A Tapestry of Light and Laughter

We stitched up our dreams with glitter and cheer,
Each patch a giggle, each knot a dear year.
With twinkling lights draped around our heads,
We prance like elves, using pillows for beds!

The dog chewed the tinsel, oh what a sight,
As we slurped on our drinks, bubbling with light.
We make silly faces in photos galore,
For laughter's the tune we love to adore!

Wrapped in our blankets, we snuggle so tightly,
Reading old stories with voices so sprightly.
The night turns to magic, our hearts dance and sway,
In this joyful tapestry, we'll always stay!

So here's to the laughter, the joy that we find,
In each silly moment, we're perfectly aligned.
With light in our hearts, we'll cherish the muse,
And weave together a world we won't refuse!

Whispered Secrets of the Snow

In the nighttime cold, we hear a cheer,
Snowmen gossiping, 'Hurry, bring the beer!'
Snowflakes waltz, like they own the stage,
While kids skate by, fueling the rage.

Cocoa in hand, we laugh at the chill,
Sledding down hills, no time to be still.
Hot chocolate spills, on a brand-new coat,
Dad falls face-first, gives the snowman a moat.

The crisp air carries a wild delight,
As squirrels debate who will steal the light.
Frosty and friends have a ball, they say,
Making snow angels while hippos still play.

All around, a giggle hides in the frost,
Whispered secrets shared, not a moment lost.
Though winter may bite, we'll dance in delight,
With each snowy flake, we embrace the night.

The Embrace of Light in Dark Times

In the dark of the night, a bulb goes out,
The dog chewed the wire, there's no need to pout.
We gather 'round candles, our spirits ignite,
Who knew a blackout could bring such delight?

Then comes the cat, like a thief in the night,
Pawing the presents, oh what a sight!
With ribbons and bows wrapped around his tail,
He's the new Santa—oh, how we'll regale!

Laughter rings loud as the shadows dance,
In a room full of people, we take a chance.
We tell silly stories, our hearts feel so bright,
To shine in the midnight, we'll make it all right.

With flashlights aglow, we create a parade,
Pirate hats on, our fears start to fade.
A night full of giggles, who knew we could climb?
In shadows we found, our own sense of rhyme.

Flickering Flames of Togetherness

Cinnamon scents waft through the air,
Uncles are lost, but who really cares?
Grandma's old recipe, a dash of wild,
Burnt cookies galore—who knew sweet could be mild?

Around the bright fire, we all come alive,
The warmth of each story helps us all thrive.
With marshmallows roasting and laughter so near,
We toast to the moments that bring us good cheer.

Socks are mismatched, but no one will judge,
We twirl in our jammies; oh, what a grudge!
Santa's got tricks up his fluffy old sleeve,
While we prank each other, there's nothing to grieve.

Together we gleam, a family so bright,
As the flames dance gently, we'll last through the night.
With silly old tales and some songs that we sing,
Flickering flames hold all our joy in their wing.

A Journey into Warmth and Light

Bundled up tight in a big, funny coat,
Parents are fretting, 'That hat's not a boat!'
With each step outside, we sprout like a tree,
Unruly and funny, we're wild and carefree.

The paths are a maze, each corner a laugh,
Snowball fights break out, oh do we chase after!
While snowflakes tickle, we roll and we play,
All our giggles echo through the grand array.

Inside, there's a feast, of pie and of cake,
But first, a few bites of the cookies we bake.
Grandpa's sweet stories are always a hit,
As we gather around, and just won't ever quit.

A journey we take in this warm, cozy scene,
With love in each corner, the best you can glean.
As laughter collides, we'll conquer the night,
With hope in our hearts, it'll all be alright.

The Warmth of Reflection and Renewal

In the glow of twinkling lights,
We all gather for festive bites.
Grandma's fruitcake takes the stage,
Even the dog runs off in a rage.

Merry moments, silly cheer,
Unwrapping gifts with holiday fear.
What's this? Socks or a tie?
Oh well, let's just let out a sigh.

Neighbors peeking, what a sight!
"Is that a tree, or a monster's height?"
Laughter echoes, spirits rise,
As we dodge the Christmas flies!

Later, we count the cookies left,
Did we eat them all, or just be deft?
Resolutions in the air,
Perhaps next year, we'll try to share!

Illuminated Dreams on Silver Nights

Under stars that seem to wink,
We roast marshmallows, let them sink.
Hot cocoa spills upon my shirt,
At least it hides the chocolate dirt!

A snowman with a lopsided grin,
Wears my scarf that looks akin.
With a carrot nose that's rather round,
I should've called that bunny hound!

Lucy's singing off-key tunes,
Even the cat howls at the moons.
We dance, we jig, we fall, we laugh,
What else to do but split the half?

Dreams of sugar plums are here,
Though it's cookies we all hold dear.
With every cheer that fills the night,
Joy says, "Hold tight to your delight!"

Magi's Blessing in the Midnight Quiet

Three wise men stargazing bright,
Brought gifts for the silent night.
But one lost his way at dawn,
Now searches for his lucky lawn.

Balthazar's map was quite a flop,
He thought he'd gift a giant mop.
Instead, we wrapped it with some flair,
And laughed as it sat in the square.

Every candle flickers and shakes,
As the cat plots its next mistakes.
Followed by the sound of a crash,
Oh dear, the ornaments in a flash!

So here's to the gifts that go astray,
To the laughter that fills our day.
For in each blunder, we find pure glee,
And joy dances wild, oh can't you see?

A Shining Star Over Peaceful Hearts

A star that shines upon the town,
Lights up faces, no one frowns.
We gather 'round with chubby cheeks,
Sharing tales, while laughter peaks.

Cookies crumble with each cheer,
As we spin 'round like we're in a sphere.
Mom's pie rests in velvet glow,
But who's the one who ate it? Oh no!

Songs of old fill up the air,
Even if the notes don't really care.
We sing about the snowman's plight,
Who lost his hat in a pillow fight!

Through giggles, warmth, and gentle peace,
We find our joy will never cease.
With shining hearts, we raise a toast,
To the silly things we cherish most!

Luminous Hearts in Frosty Air

In the chilly air, we dance with glee,
Wearing socks that don't quite match, you see!
Snowmen wave with carrot noses wide,
While we laugh and trip, with holiday pride.

Reindeer hats on heads just look so neat,
But the ears flop down, oh, what a feat!
Our mugs are filled with cocoa so sweet,
Though one spills fast - a comedy heat!

Wishing flakes twirl as kids shout 'hooray!'
Then slip on ice in an awkward ballet.
The mischief grows as lights start to twinkle,
And everyone's jolly, not one heart's a wrinkle.

Toasting with cookies, we chomp and chew,
While grandma giggles at the chaos we brew.
All around us, warmth takes its flight,
In a season where everyone feels just right.

The Glow of Kindness

The cat's in the tree, a sight to behold,
As we gather 'round stories from times of old.
Grandpa's tall tales of the holiday cheer,
Have us rolling with laughter, oh dear, oh dear!

Baking cookies, flour in the air,
It's a sweet disaster, an absent-minded affair.
With sprinkles gone wild, they're all out of sight,
Yet the smiles on our faces shine oh so bright.

The wish list is scribbled with doodles and glee,
"Santa, please bring me a parakeet tree!"
With every giggle, the spirits rise high,
As we present gifts to the dog, who can't lie.

So here's to the love that sparkles and glows,
To the joy that within every laughter flows.
Celebrate silly, for here's what we know:
Kindness and humor make the warmest show!

Lanterns of the Longest Night

As darkness wraps tight like a silly old blanket,
With lanterns aglow, what mischief you can make it!
Children's footsteps crunch on the frosty ground,
While giggles and whispers of joy can be found.

Twinkling lights tangle, a festive dread,
We laugh at the trouble while wearing our thread.
The cat suddenly leaps, a shadow, a race,
Knocking over decorations with great clumsy grace.

Now, carols are sung in a truly mad way,
Off-key but so happy, in a jolly array.
We jostle and jingle with bells in our boot,
Making spirits brighter with every reprute.

The night stretches on with stars in a fight,
Who can shine brightest? Oh, what a delight!
Gather all close, we'll weather this test,
With lanterns of laughter, we'll shine at our best!

Beneath the Mistletoe Magic

Underneath the branches, a kiss gone wrong,
As Uncle Joe's laughter breaks out like a song.
With mistletoe dangling above the dog's head,
He sneezes and wags—what happened? Who said red?

The stockings are hung without much of flair,
With pet hair and tinsel all weighing the air.
We gather for games, where chaos ensues,
And Aunt Sue's board game has only lost clues!

The air is too rich with the smell of delight,
As cookies are baked in the glow of the night.
But sprinkles fly high like confetti on snow,
Creating a charm that only we know!

So let's toast with hot chocolate, spill a bit too,
Laughter and love are the gifts we are due.
Under the mistletoe, all worries take flight,
It's the joy of togetherness that feels just right!

When Stars Paint the Sky

When stars paint the sky like a toddler's art,
We giggle and dance, a light-hearted start.
With ornaments twinkling just like our grins,
And reports of bright reindeer, where do we begin?

The snowmen are frowning, their nose all askew,
While penguins un-giftwrap, in their tuxedos too.
A chorus of laughter as they trip on the ice,
Who knew winter joy included such spice?

With cocoa in hand, we share silly tales,
Of elves in yoga pants, outsmarting the gales.
They tangle the tinsel, creating a mess,
But we all laugh along; it's simply the best!

So raise up your glasses, let the laughter soar,
As we dance with the stars and open the door.
To moments of joy, to fun without bound,
In this wild tapestry, together we're found.

Embracing Solstice's Glow

As winter creeps in, with its frosty embrace,
We gather 'round fires, all smiling with grace.
The nights are long, but our spirits take flight,
With puns and hot chocolate, we savor the night.

A gnome on the shelf gives a wink and a grin,
He sneaks lots of cookies, oh where to begin?
His buddy the reindeer is dancing around,
With snowflakes as sequins, spreading joy all around.

The lights in the windows are twinkling so bright,
Competing with laughter, a truly fine sight.
We sing silly carols, not caring who's near,
With rhythms so wobbly, we spread the cheer.

So here's to the moments that light up the dark,
Where jokes and warm hugs ignite our own spark.
As we share in our love, may the good times prevail,
In the glow of the solstice, let's dance without fail!

The Promise of New Beginnings

With the dawn of great hopes, resolutions we make,
To dance with the ducks and eat lots of cake.
The calendar flips, it's chaos, it's fun,
We'll gamble on diets but still weigh a ton.

The snowman looks on as we shrug off our fears,
While sipping hot cider and crazy ideas.
We might try new hobbies, like knitting a scarf,
But end up with socks that are really quite zarff.

With glitter and baubles, we dream of the year,
Of all the great things that will soon bring us cheer.
We'll laugh at our blunders, our whims and our quests,
In the circus of life, we're all just jesters dressed.

Embracing the chaos, we jump with delight,
For every new sunrise brings the promise of light.
So let's raise our voices and toast to the spree,
Together we'll wander and be ever free!

Shimmering Hope in the Cold

When the chill in the air starts to play with our nose,
We wrap up in blankets, in comfort we doze.
The flickers of laughter are warming our hearts,
As we plan silly snowball dart-throwing arts.

The icicles dangle, like teeth of a beast,
While penguins skate by, making snowmen at least.
We chuckle and giggle at snowflakes so grand,
Who knew winter wonders could all be so planned?

With lights that are twinkling like stars made of cheer,
We dance in the glow, throughout this brave year.
Where wishes are wrapped up in humor and fun,
In a world spun with magic, we dance 'til we're done.

So here's to the laughter, the joy and the bliss,
May our hearts be so light, it's hard to miss.
In the tales that we share and the memories bold,
We weave together the shimmering hope in the cold.

Milton Keynes UK
Ingram Content Group UK Ltd.
UKHW021241191124
451300UK00007B/180

9 789916 940402